Green Roses Bloom for Icarus

Poems

Hiromi Yoshida

ROADSIDE PRESS

Green Roses Bloom for Icarus
Copyright © Hiromi Yoshida, 2024
ISBN: 979-8-9902309-4-1

Cover design based on the Icarus illustration by Walter Crane (1845-1915)
Editor: Michele McDannold

Roadside Press
Colchester, Illinois

For Timothy M. Prehn, MIS
(1970–2015)

Seraphic Cheerleader

Contents

Icarus | Epicanthus

Icarus Redux

ACKNOWLEDGMENTS

Throughout *Green Roses Bloom for Icarus*, the mythic Icarus is the floating signifier of desire that circulates among us, and whose meaning and value fluctuate arbitrarily. Thus, Icarus is the superseded superstar, the haunting specter, and the symptom of our collective disease, like a randomly floating coronavirus particle. Icarus is also, a bad penny (or its flipside, corroded obverse), a flipped bird, an obscene signifier—hermaphroditic diva, and graffiti scrawl.
To extricate ourselves from the circuitry of desire that the fall of Icarus catalyzed, we celebrate the green rose, the symbol of emerging art in James Joyce's *A Portrait of the Artist as a Young Man*. Celebration converts the green of copper corrosion, of self-corrupting envy, into the green of lyric seabloom and redemptive hope. Thus, Icarus plunges into the sea of green roses, only to be resurrected endlessly.

For enabling *Green Roses Bloom for Icarus*, I thank the following editors and publishers.
Firstly, many thanks to Rodger Moody at Silverfish Review Press; and to Kelli Russell Agodon and Annette Spaulding-Convy at Two Sylvias Press for selecting *Green Roses Bloom for Icarus* as a semifinalist for the 2020 Gerald Cable Book Award, and for the 2018 Wilder Series Poetry Book Prize respectively.

Grateful acknowledgment is made to the editors of these publications in which these poems first appeared, sometimes in different versions.

Alien Buddha Zine, "Green Pennies," "Iconic Things," "Sylvia's Miscarriage," "Japanese Idols," "Bikini Body," "The Date (August 7, 1930)"
Bathtub Gin, "Icarus Burning"

The Beatnik Cowboy, "Cheese Icarus"

Borderline, "Speaking for Edvard Munch's *The Sin*" (reprinted in *They Call Us*)

Discover Nikkei Journal, "Godwind," "Umami"

Evening Street Review, "TV Dinner"

Evergreen Review, "Thanksgiving 2003"

Flying Island Journal, "Shikata ga Nai (Let It Be)," Hiroshima & Nagasaki," "After the Fire"

Gidra, "Grandmother's Kitchen," "COVID America"

Indiana Voice Journal, "Dumpster Diving," "Last Supper in Terre Haute"

The Indianapolis Review, "Mother of Icarus," "Icarus | Epicanthus," "Bachelor Party"

Last Stanza Poetry Journal, "Rapunzel," "Paper Doll," "Say Her Asian Name"

New Generation Beats 2023 Anthology, "Last Lunch in Littleton, Colorado"

Plath Profiles, "Realia"

The Power of the Feminine "I" Anthology, "Speaking for Edvard Munch's *The Sin*," "Speaking for William Holman Hunt's *The Lady of Shalott*," "Juliet in the Crypt"

The Rain, Party, & Disaster Society, "Icarus Redux," "The Iconization of Rosa Parks"

The Rise Up Review, "Ferguson, Missouri (August 2014)"

The Ryder Magazine, "Shrove Tuesday"

SAVOR: Poems for the Tongue, "Grandmother's Kitchen"

Work Literary Magazine, "The Exotic Dancer"

Additional thanks to the Indiana Arts Commission, the Indiana State Library, and the Office of the Indiana Poet Laureate for including in the INverse Poetry Archive "Last Supper in Terre Haute."

My gratitude extends to Finishing Line Press for the chapbooks *Icarus Burning* (2020) and

Epicanthus (2021), and to Alien Buddha Press for *Icarus Redux* (2021) and *Icarus Superstar* (2023) in which these poems appear, sometimes in different versions:

Icarus Burning: "Icarus Burning," "The Exotic Dancer," "The Exotic Dance Club Patron," "Speaking for Edvard Munch's The Sin," "Realia," "The Doll," "Duck, Duck, Goose," "'Wanted,'" "Icarus Redux," "The Iconization of Rosa Parks"

Epicanthus: "Godwind," "Moon Palace King," "Shikata ga Nai (Let It Be)," "Hiroshima & Nagasaki," "Gas Panic," "Empire State Building Soup," "TV Dinner," "Channel Surfers," "Grandmother's Kitchen," "Umami," "COVID America"

Icarus Redux: "Green Pennies," "Iconic Things," "Realia," "'Wanted,'" "Gargoyle," "Icarus Redux," "Thanksgiving 2003," "Last Supper in Terre Haute," "Gunshot," "Archived Realia in Littleton, Colorado," "The Iconization of Rosa Parks," "COVID America"

Icarus Superstar: "East Village Breakfast," "1970s NYC Subway Graffiti," "NYC Subway Map," "Nixon Crying on Color TV," "D-Train Beggar," "Cheap Champagne," "The Receptionist," "Lunch Break," "Night Landing at LaGuardia Airport," "Car Burning on the Cross Bronx Expressway," "Bling," "Icarus Superstar," "Icarus Ekphrasis," "Piss Icarus," "Paper Doll," "Icarus Hermaphrodite," "Mother of Icarus," "Icarus Penis," "Icarus | Epicanthus," "Icarus Obverse"

My deepest thanks to Jenny Kalahar for the *Last Stanza Poetry Journal* Editor's Choice Award for "Say Her Asian Name," and these editors for their nominations: Red Focks at Alien Buddha Press, "COVID America," 2021 Pushcart Prize; Mary Brown at *Flying Island Journal*, "After the Fire," 2020 Best of the Net.

For their friendship, the supporting drive behind *Green Roses Bloom for Icarus*, I thank members of the Writers Guild at Bloomington, most especially, Tony Brewer, Joan Hawkins, Kyle Quass,

April Ridge, and Molly Gleeson. My appreciation extends to Patsy Rahn, James Dorr, and Antonia Matthew, original Guild members, for their warm continuing support. I also thank Mary M. Brown and Marjie Giffin at *Flying Island Journal*. For other literary arts opportunities and experiences, I thank Rosaleen Crowley at Brick Street Poetry, Inc.; Henry Leck at the Arts Alliance of Greater Bloomington; Luann Johnson at WFIU; Ron Eid at *Limestone Post Magazine*; Chaz Mo at the City of Bloomington; and Nancy Bombaci at Mitchell College.

Special thanks to Jonathan S Baker for inspiring my most recent Icarus poems. More thanks to C. S. Mathews for giving me the thumbs-up to use her "Icarus Suicide" artwork title for the poem that made it into this collection. Thanks to both of them for producing *Icarus Hieroglyph* for The Grind Stone chapbook series, and for featuring me at the Poetry Speaks reading series at the Bokeh Lounge, Evansville, Indiana.

For other poetic license antics, I thank Rachel Smith, Bloomington's GNO wonderwoman.

Deepest love and thanks to my mother, Dr. Toyoko Yoshida, fellow witness of overflowing ashcans from which Icarus is ceaselessly resurrected.

Thanks to everybody who stood with me to watch the rise and fall of Icarus—his "coin-sized overreach" toward the greening sun.

Icarus Burning

Icarus Burning

The Aztec heart of the sun blazes a rush hour trail of amniotic blood
                        across skyscraping altars of plexiglass horizons

shimmering in the golden crucible of salt-licked Red Seatides
and questions pickled in formaldehyde jars

X-rated carbon copies of bones bleaching on perforated clotheslines

twisting a ticker tape dance through the magnetic plush
of anemone fingers reaching into oversized manila envelopes

(sanctified valentine
in utero extremis).

The seedy pulp of sunflowering high noons in boxed lunch offices
with redflowering sushi and lacquerware
sticking the polluted pollen of viscous heart—
epithelial kimono silk—dilating to dimensions of premature prognosis—

the broken beat of time, measured in silver teaspoons
of nauseating ether—and the siren song of drowning mermaids
                        embroidering the counterfeit goldrush fringe

of stock exchanges—coin-sized overreach toward the numb vanishing

                point of decimated dollars and decapitated cents.

And Icarus minted in accolades of green—
plunging into the copperplate sea of acidic tears—waxing toward the boiling
point on the Hudson horizon of disheveled trees in Riverside Park—
of sinking suns and new moons giving new birth to the fallen

stars and the debris of night, the harlot's jewelcase flung open

                at the neon feet of commuters surging through the turnstiles—

                roiling mass of Nikes and rollerblades and Evian limbs

winging home on spiked Gatorade.

Deli lights splintering

through the fluorescent eyes of the nymphomaniac caravan
needling through the needy night murmurous with the junky scrawl of graffiti incantations rumbling
through the groins of iconoclastic acolytes—

green with gangrenous envy and burning bile, the new apocalypse
squeezing through the tinfoiled undergarments of transvestites chewing on
tinsel gumwrappers and gunshot wounds—
bleeding a stigmata of spare change and jangling eyes,
begging the bony hand to cast a
jaundiced benediction of swiney

pearls twining rosary beads of perspiration through the tangled traffic of
funereal arteries oozing green blood and light through the Eustachian
tunnels and the blood-

shot eye vessels blinking on jewelstrung highways and AM radio
static crackling through the dark of flying night at Ground
Zero below sea level.

Godwind

The planes deliberately collided into the World
Trade Center, North and South Towers,
like steel-winged Icarus, twinned, burning—

kamikaze crash and decimation—the shredded paper gods shedding green
    pennies and white hair—the Manhattan skyline was a smoggy plexiglass
altar where dreams were
                sacrificed to the rising sun (that smirking bastard). Pedestrians coughed, gagged on

the foretaste of phoenix ash; black stench
of needless apocalypse clogged
    nostrils—resurrection an unwritten blueprint drifting on wayward
godwind—

East Village Breakfast

"You look like you want
to throw up," he said
to me, as I stared at the egg yolk streaks across my thick, greasy
diner plate. I could've

reached across our table for a discarded
crust of toast to dabble in the yellow grease to produce
an oil painting of the murky horizon—spilled the cold

flavorless coffee from my saucer for
watercolor effect; salt and pepper would've enhanced the grainy
texture; ketchup dislodged from
        the asphyxiated glass bottle neck bloodying the horizon to
        produce the fingerpainted twilight when nymphomaniacal
        New York City shades emerge from office cubicles, subway cars,
        studio apartment lofts, and diner booths

in a rush hour carnival of neon fluorescence—
devouring plexiglass, swallowing swiney
pearls bubbling through cheap champagne bottles. I was

his residue of sex addict desire, wanting to expel
from my snaky, undernourished body the bleached

memory of the night before our compulsory

        breakfast—stringing together each night after the first

        like aligning fake pearls for a harlot's G-string—

repetition compulsion to circumvent the

        one-night stand stigma of the shudder of premature

        orgasm on a cheap Sears mattress in a South Bronx apartment;

messy circumambulation round dumpsters over-

        flowing shattered Rolling Rock bottles, used Trojans, discarded coffee grinds, unopened

ketchup packets—egg yolk oozing from cracked shells in cardboard cartons—

swine breeding in roaring sanitation trucks, and Icarus

falling beyond the Hudson horizon.

1970s NYC Subway Graffiti

Insert tarnished tokens into wooden,
orange paint flaking
turnstile slots—rush into subway cars, where
loopy, fuzzy, hieroglyphic
graffiti had infiltrated like psychedelic
mildew of the acid-tripping mind—
rattling, roaring down black tunnels toward the Bronx Zoo,
                      Central Park, Coney Island, Wall Street,
Greenwich Village, Chinatown, Times Square, Port Authority, Grand
Central—eastside, westside, northbound, southbound,
                      crisscrossing red, green, blue, orange, yellow,
purple, brown lines like varicose veins across the harlot junkie body of
New York City—

the subway ride in the 1970s was an underground explosion of
cartographic colors—psychedelic graffiti scrawl swallowed into
Eustachian dark, then, vomited into blazing light at the end of the
tunnel.

NYC Subway Map

Consider the lines crisscrossing beneath
cracked plexiglass in New York City subway cars—
the Bronx being the city's disheveled head; Manhattan, its slanting
torso; Staten Island, its

     webbed foot soaking in New York Harbor; Brooklyn and
Queens, additional body parts—

     dismembered like brown gingerbread cookie fragments.
Consider Icarus caught in the

intricate webwork of subway lines—sunbaked boy sprouting green
wings—falling into New York Harbor—gingerly minted and
replicated.

Nixon Crying on Color TV

Crocodile tears—psychedelic ooze,
every channel the same, Nixon crying on each
flashing screen of newly manufactured color TVs
in America. Water Gate unleashed the floodgates of dirty laundry
water—the American dream corroding greenly
like Abe Lincoln's profile on tarnished pennies.

Static buzz of lime green, magenta, yellow—
drip of rainbow tears and grinning crocodiles. I was

that New York City child approaching ten,
wondering why this man was crying on every single
cable TV channel; why my family didn't have a color
TV yet; why I needed to say good-bye
to a lost America.

D-Train Beggar

Green pennies jangling
in the plastic cup
clutched in the scrawny
black hand of
the blind D-train beggar
tapping by us with his cane—
on our way to the Lincoln Center for the Performing Arts,
                       standing room tickets to *Siegfried* in my
beaded purse. Our animated talk halted,
and my date retained his respectful silence
                       long after the beggar had staggered by us—
the dark subway roar down Eustachian corridors obliterating the need
to keep talking till the
                       shuddering blaze of lights at the end of
the tunnel at 59th Street, Columbus Circle.

The Exotic Dancer

She undulates a cocaine dream,
psychopomp of dry-iced
cocktails, salted
rocks &
splin-
　　tered chandelier nights.

She draws rhinestone accolades—
sticky shot glass
pennies &
overstuffed dollars from hoodwinked
snakeskin wallets in crinkled

Armani pants,
lapdancing private
peek-a-boo booths of
beaded curtain tricks spilling
champagne buckets &
mirrored silver—
spitting out pomegranate
seeds from between
tiny porcelain teeth at
gargoyle stevedores

ogling painted caravans &
copping a Coptic
animadversion—

shedding flimsy wrap-
around skirts &
polyester lace bra
straps to a mere
G-string of scaly gorgon eyes
   glittering hard
    sequins
    at tassled
    ballerina
    antics

twisting a tourniquet of
trapeze tulle &
tight fishnet round &
round a flaccid drum
delirium—
spinning acrobatic
tilting a dizzy
high-rise axis toward a
levity of gyrating
Jerusalems.

Castaway snake
goddess, she
writhes beneath
disenchanted moons—

her calculated striptease
catalyzing a litany of

Village junkies
plastic saints
ex-communicated *mater dolorosas*
nymphomaniacal hermaphrodites
dungeon damsels with dagger eyes &
bearded hipsters.

Queen of orgiastic limbo,
she staggers into
Grand Central Station—
vomiting a

sequence of swiney pearls,
high-strung on
cheap champagne.

Cheap Champagne

Allegedly, his oil shares in Texas, had made him
the pampered millionaire
at the Kit Kat Klub, where he ordered
overpriced, dubious champagne (they were out
of Dom Pérignon)—swiney pearls bubbling
out of his frothy, replenished glass. He

stared at the puddle on the round Formica
table waxing into the gold sea, where he saw Venus rising like a
                              premature hard-on, smirking over her

alabaster shoulder, replicating the orchestrated
choreography of topless dancers gyrating on the vast tinseled stage
before him. The pimping manager
and the fake-blonde hostesses
milked him like the obese
golden calf till he slumped
backward in his tilting chair, inert
mountain of flabby greying flesh; the plump

expert cocktail waitress, concerned
she might never receive the fistful of hundred-dollar bills
she'd expected for her service—the green numbers sliding down her

chunky sequined legs into the Times Square sewers standing in for the open mouths of swine breeding in the Kit Kat Klub's over-flowing cash registers.

The Exotic Dance Club Patron

I saw him,
sitting alone,
at the Kit Kat Klub bar, his back
turned toward the vast tinseled stage where

pale, young,
vulnerable dancers
shed plaid wrap-
around skirts
and polyester
bras. He was

my dream guy
in the underworld of live
adult entertainment
on W. 43rd St. near
Times Square; between Hell's
Kitchen and the Garment District.

Unlikely hipster
patron, his dark
eyes gazed at melting ice
cubes in

the unreplenished
glass before him. I

broke his trance—
a disarmed
enchantress, cock-
tail waitress novice;
I'd forgotten
to order the designated
overpriced crap
champagne from the
frowning bartender
who snarled,

"What would you like to drink?"
—the patron being expected
to pay, and I, his pimped

server to follow the scripted sequence: sip, spit, smile—
the champagne being orally
transferred to the frosted
glass simulating water chaser—
as though champagne needs to be chased by anything other than its own
effervescence.

We agreed to meet up, after I'd clocked out of
the Kit Kat Klub. I
didn't bother to claim
the night's wages, and he
didn't show up. Instead,

I've remembered him,
    a shadow shivering along Times Square sidewalks,
        blinking into neon graffiti—

an angelic scrawl across smoggy New York City skies.

The Receptionist

The high-pitched gasp (subdued
scream) disrupted drowsy post-
lunch quietude at the magazine
publishing office. The CEO

coughed, adjusted his spectacles:
"Everybody, stay calm!" he
urged assembled staff outside my
workspace, when none
of us had uttered one
word.   The quiet
                  Black receptionist had approached
the vivacious white editorial assistant's
             cubicle with a knife, prior to the former's removal
to a psych ward.   The glint on the invisible knife's edge

emerged into that afternoon's
sun glare into which Icarus had flown—a dark speck upon the expiring
horizon.

Lunch Break

She was
that quiet, soft-spoken
Black receptionist—breaking
the monotony of solitary
lunches that one afternoon she
invited me to join her. Welcome

change from my own
solitary lunches at the vast
unoccupied university commons lounge
when I was the Dean of Students receptionist;
chance to upgrade

my homemade egg salad sandwiches
to midtown Manhattan deli takeout:
bowtie pasta tossed in pesto sauce; sliced tomatoes
and mozzarella cheese marinated in
balsamic vinegar and olive oil,
speckled with basil leaves—crammed into Styrofoam
clamshell boxes, while she

produced her modest
Tupperware leftovers from the night

before. We blinked in the Central Park sunlight,
her barely audible voice seemed to emanate from
the sidewalk shadows we cast at our

awkward, shuffling feet.   She
never mentioned the snide remarks,
the insolent glances she might've endured
from the white editorial assistant, who
          stalked by her solitary receptionist desk at 9:00 AM and
5:00 PM each day—
smirking past her with her white female colleague.   She was

the equal opportunity poster child,
the tall blonde Midwestern CEO secretary
being the workplace supermodel, who monopolized
the photocopy machine, the petite Filipina accountant,
her sidekick (like Ginger and Mary Ann). They were

tacitly complicit, too, neither of them glancing at the Black
receptionist, who had been invisible like her entire race—
till her final solitary
lunch hour when the impulse had coalesced
in her empty belly—the askew
sunlight glinted off the knife she wielded, as she glided toward the
hated cubicle—

and Icarus fell into the Hudson River, a green
millstone round the necks of
New York City workers, empty clamshell boxes
yawning in overflowing dumpsters.

Night Landing at LaGuardia Airport

Beyond the aircraft
window, pinpoint lights
stud the dark of flying night—
wax into a sea of rhinestones
and sequins—hard glitter of harlot eyes,
and jewel-strung highways and bridges—
blurring into the black sheet of water
approaching closer, and
closer beneath my aircraft seat—and after the twitch of steel wings,
and the turbine engine's orgasmic
                shudder, the wheels glide across the unlikely tarmac,
and the landing
is perfected.

Car Burning on the Cross Bronx Expressway

The commuter van shuttling between university campuses
                              offered passengers thrilling escapes from the
south Bronx to midtown Manhattan—

past the abandoned, crumbling, gutted tenements,
bleak housing projects, graffiti murals of municipal basketball courts—
                              the loose-limbed Black boys shrugging, ambling
by—green pennies jangling
                              in their homeboy pants pockets—till the van
sped down the Cross Bronx Expressway, and slackened to a halt
alongside a blazing vehicle;

sidling past it in a dense grey fog of carbon monoxide, the van became
a red ant in a surrealist oil painting—crawling past the viscously
                              greening trees of Riverside Park along the
roiling Hudson River.

Green Pennies

While the earth was tilting on its axis, and the Berlin Wall was collapsing,
and time zones were changing—

pennies were oxidizing in unreachable corners beneath
our living room sofas—green flush of envy (or some other

equally corrosive emotion) spreading across Abe Lincoln's coppery
countenance like some gangrenous disease—catalyzing once again the
endless circulation of tarnished currency.

Iconic Things

Sylvia Plath's archived hair
Elvis Presley's performance guitars
Andy Warhol's Campbell soup cans
Marilyn Monroe's superannuated gowns

the spongy gold meat of Hostess Twinkies
the sun that killed Icarus @ high noon
shiny things of fluctuating
economic value—

These iconic things keep
their bling zing, unlike the

pomegranate seeds
Persephone in Hades spits

out.

Bling

zing! zing!

bling! bling!

The sun is the thing
        beyond the reach of Icarus—sullen gold eyeball,
        surly contestant of constellations, glowering at the blinging
sky.

zing! zing!

The sky is the thing,
        ozone dome, whose depletion threatens extinction of
        all the lovely green phenomena stirring on earth, ecstatic.

bling! bling!

The American Dream is the thing (ultimate fling)—
        cash registers overflow green pennies—they roll into
unreachable crevices

beneath overstuffed sofas—

blinging.

ringing.

singing.

Icarus Superstar

No longer the most distant
star from Earth—superseded
by Earendel, newly discovered. Yet,

Icarus remains
burning, a
blue supergiant,
larger and
brighter than the sun—

billions of light years away
from our blinking
eyes, unexpired specter.

Green Icarus slides into
           blue along the slippery light spectrum—waxing
toward red light districts of the mind reimagining corroded
        pennies.   Superstardom was

within Icarus' coin-sized overreach till he became
the flipped bird
itself (subversive, obscene
signifier), drowning in the green

sea of envy, a superseded, scratched-
out asterisk.

Icarus Ekphrasis

Icarus Ekphrasis

In Louis Parsons' oil painting,
Icarus is already a ghost—
a white chalky form floating against
a night blue sky bleeding pink
rose petals and pearling stars—
scratching away paintbrush errors
and after-thoughts beneath
dense layers of roiling
blue and rust-colored paint—
earth-colored wings to gird
the ghost bleeding his way out of Crete
before the cruel sunrise,
and the secret greening of
Aegean sea waves curling into frothy
roses beneath the ghostly
feet; pale vertical streaks streaming
from oversized wings, viscous
tears and eye wax; a flutter of
eyelashes and startled birds.

Speaking for Edvard Munch's *The Sin*

I am your sin
long-haired woman
coiling serpent
praises round
your throat: I cling
to you like the fragrance
you wear compulsively
without my consent.
I am the carbon
monoxide your rattling
ribcage exhales; the jeweled
oxymoron; thorn in the flesh
of your Achilles heel,
your frailty housed
in treacherous nunnery
dark after vespers
evaporate a catacomb
stench of bones &
memories of how
you masturbated on full
moon nights like a silly
bleached vampire.

Darling, I am
your wide-eyed sin—
growing unkempt
secrets behind your
eyelids, the dirt in your
fingernails, the piss in your
pants, the garlic
nymph reeking
formaldehyde.

Speaking for William Holman Hunt's *The Lady of Shalott*

I would never have looked at
you if I knew looks could kill (quite
literally). But you invaded my claustrophobic
mirror space and screwed up
my weaving without requesting the
requisite permission to do so. Unlike Penelope, I

can't pick up from where I'd left
off—just to redo my maidenly handiwork again and again—
endlessly like a mad lyric refrain that won't
observe STOP signs at each designated intersection—instead moving inexorably and tortuously
toward the obvious narrative resolution of happily-ever-after with the shimmering mail-armored dude
and his white hobby-horse.

So, cast your piercing
glance at me, Lance—see me tangled up like a
spider in its own nefarious web—the silken threads tightly twisting into a

peacock-colored straitjacket—hair floating like a
              second web in all directions—charged with electric static like you'd touched a
barbed wire nerve in me that back-

fired, barbecuing me (not you), in sizzle dazzle apocalyptic splendor.
At least I'll look pretty when I'm dead.

Juliet in the Crypt

My lips part
for oxygen in the Capulet crypt,
where I'm out of context
among cobwebbed skulls. Still,

the folds of my gown invite
mildew molecules—greenly (envious
movement). My

eyelids flutter open; pins and
needles tingle through limp
hands and feet; the vermilion
sheath for the "happy

dagger" opens, a dusty rosebud; I
yawn in dying
flambeaux light. Oh, Romeo!
Is that you, twitching
at my tingling
feet?

Rapunzel

It all began with desire for lettuce—
even the stolen variety
would do for her—
strange, uncontrollable pregnancy cravings—
                      driving her to the ragged edge
of the precipice of no certain return. Did she

ever suspect the witch would hoodwink her—
snatch away from her the rosy child
like an innocent cabbage (even
before it had been weaned from its mother's

heavy, milk-laden
breasts)? After all,

what use could the witch have had for a
golden-haired girl languidly watching suns
rise and wax and set day after day in that insular,
inaccessible tower?

Rapunzel
could have redeemed herself (if
she had only known it) with her own hands,

her own hair—by extension, her own brain
(such a blonde bimbo,
you'd think). After all, the prince was
completely useless, and what's more, extraneous (in
this narrative context), for he was no
redeemer—indeed, merely
the void that mirrored Rapunzel's [v]acuity;
            [excision of the virgin from the phallic tower
                        being the vulgar form of redemption].

"Hey, nonny, nonny…" she would sing
all day, braiding and unbraiding locks of golden hair (but never
upbraiding the witch or the prince, who were the same to her,
just that the latter could scale the tower
                        with greater, longer-legged, penised alacrity)—

"Hey, nonny, nonny, where is my Johnny?
Oh, Johnny-come-lately…"
She was a caged bird, singing
for her cold supper, waiting apathetically
for the witch to come home: "Rapunzel,
Rapunzel, let down your golden hair!"
when she had the option to refuse, knowing
            the witch had no broomstick with which to beat her into
bruised compliance.

Piss Icarus

Icarus plunges into a
vortex of amniotic fluid and formaldehyde—
drowning merboy with outspread wings, crucified,
a marinated albatross.

The roiling Aegean Sea was an oil-painted repository of flotsam and
jetsam—
     urine leaking from tight bathing trunks, and the pissed-off
centuries of centaurs galloping
     toward strange sea light—glimmer of flowering anemone—sea
waves caressing briny beaches with hoary fingers, combing tangled

mermaid hair—and Icarus drifting, suspended
     in opacity, green replica of Serrano's Christ.

Realia

Sylvia's Hair

Wavy cascade of mousy brown hair, exhibit
at the Lilly Library, invites voyeuristic
"peanut-crunching" crowds to gawk awkwardly—shorn from the
[actual] head that was

Sylvia Plath's. From papery catacombs, the realia object was
resurrected, whispering her abjected
name—Lady Lazarus, her
curvilinear remnant
fusing the golden ash, the slippery
            mirror, the Japanese moon, the paper sky—crinkling into

bone-colored preservation tissue. Castaway
snaky DNA strand of a goddess smiling
hieroglyphically at her

accomplished striptease; she
devours ether—vomiting peanut
shells, the stink of formaldehyde clinging to her
"old whore petticoats."

Sibilance

Slippery sybil,
silver sylvan sylph—
sliver of the new moon (castaway
fingernail

paring)—Sylvia sliding into new
sibilant lexicons—spitting salvia—
                savoring saliva—sidling into tight pews;

sizzling audacity,
like Electra burning;
bald-headed lightbulb,
contending
with singeing moths,
unwinged—singing unhinged songs.

Paper Doll

mouth, red wound,
wombed | un-
wombed woman,
hag witch, itchy twitch
beneath haggard wigs;
she never knew her daughter
would shrink and shrivel
into paper and paraphernalia—
sprout into the gargantuan,
gangrenous, cantankerous
canker sore of her
grimacing mouth; the in-
grown toenail; the stubborn
callus on the heart's tender
flesh, begging for the
appeasement of hungry
moths that gnaw away at her
daughter's papered edges; jagged
pink petticoat cut out
with blunt, unwieldy
scissors—Sylvia
Plath, the slippery
symptom, remnant

realia, bleached signifier—the desiccated snake gagging on
                              its endless tail—she slumbers,
smiling and accomplished,
folded away into archival boxes, out of the witch mother's
twitchy reach.

Sylvia's Miscarriage

Wet mass of fetal tissue
slipped through her [elliptical
elision]—pink cup, with no
lid, opening tulips,
suddenly shut, mouthless.

That slippage was
beaten out of her
like egg yolk (allegedly)—
streaming into the petri dish
of public scrutiny
for additional dissection;
glossy marginalia
gathered from over-
flowing archives—

question marks
unfurl red
swirls in formaldehyde
jars, bleeding fetal
onomatopoeia,
and other dyslexic
lexicons, and Sylvia's

unbaked loaves are
cold hard nunnery
tombstones in her
catacomb oven, her

tabloid story unraveling
again, feeding bread-
crumbs to voracious
media vultures.

Icarus Hermaphrodite

Sunward drifting signifier—
dust mote, or vitreous floater, before the
blinking eye—mercurial shapeshift beyond
all boiling points—hot wax oozing from the osier
framework of makeshift wings, and sudden
                    scatter of feathers across the Aegean Sea's oily
surface, greening viscously.

The sun wears a golden skirt, and Icarus is a
drowning mermaid—slippery hermaphrodite floating beyond the coin-
sized reach of obvious meaning, and corroded coppery value.

Mother of Icarus

The mother of Icarus was
effaced from the father-son narrative,
as though she didn't matter. Who
was she, who birthed that silly,
defiant boy? Who

became that scrawny
flipped bird (f-word
embodiment)? Motherless
fetus plunging into the amniotic
formaldehyde sea, now a green rose,
blooming from the splashing
dapple of the sun's coin-sized
reflection? Did the mother

of Icarus sweep up her hair in intricate
braids round her worried head each
morning before she stoked the fire
for their breakfast? Did she shatter

the earthenware pots in her over-
eagerness to serve her husband and son?

Did she bunch up her skirts around
her thick waist and wide hips
to wade in the Aegean Sea, soaking her
tired flat feet? Did she

sprout wings in the secret
dark of her own mazy mind? Did she
ossify into a crumbling
caryatid, pillar of salt? Did she

become the ball of thread
in Ariadne's hands—unraveling its
long-winded way toward liberation
from Crete? Did she

smile when green roses bloomed
for Icarus?

Father of Icarus

He sees his son soaring sunward,
while he himself flies steadily parallel with the horizon—observing the middle ground.

Glimpse of gold in the corner of his
weary eye—suddenly green and frothy, and

a dappled splash below,
the coin-sized sun's reflection rippling, blooming into a sea green rose—
that sad place where his son

fell.

The boy had slipped from his cunning, dexterous hands
like Pasiphaë's loose-limbed doll.   Icarus was

the jointed, anointed one, a
vague smudge on an oily canvas, his
pasty white feet its paintless speck—that waxy residue in bloodshot eyes.   Daedalus
               lands on the sunless coast, folding away his makeshift
wings, stroking his briny beard, dreaming of gathering the green roses that bloomed where his
               son had made that big splash   without his consent.

Icarus Penis

Floating signifier threatened with castration—
What shiny thing lurks
beneath the sun's gold skirt?

Icarus, sad penis,
premature ejaculation residue—
Lacanian Phallus shriveled
into a castaway fingernail paring—
drowning in the Aegean Sea
with mermaids exchanging fishtails for
flat feet—scales falling
from burnt eyeballs
too late. Aphrodite

springs upward—
a seafoam column from the green place
where Icarus drowned—
hermaphroditically.

Gargoyle

Grey grimacing mouth—
vomiting rainwater gurgling toward
                          toppling tombstones, mud-spattered,
awaiting the erosion of years. Grotesque

stonework coalesced from
copulation of imp, griffin, and ugly
unwinged cherub—unholy ménage-à-trois;
the bulging eyeballs in the demon face
glance toward curlicued clouds on the blunt horizon,
                          a luminous knife edge cutting into the fallow
land below.

The gargoyle leers,
chagrin of seraphim, pride of baroque
cathedral years—an obscene gloss
                          in the luminous landscape's intricate
marginalia.

Icarus Before the Fall

Did he watch the strange seabirds pass over
     the isle of Crete—yearning to emulate their long wayward flight?

Did he skip flat stones across the unruly, murky surface of the Aegean Sea,
     contemplating the next sullen supper of unleavened bread and charred meat?

Did he watch his father sweating in his workshop, bending osier
     strips into strange compliance—shift his bored gaze toward Pasiphaë's painted dolls?

Did he hum wordless ditties, replicating the buzz of flies
     that speckled his dinner plate?

Did he press a conch shell to his tingling ear, hearkening to
     the soft roar of predestination?

Did his driftwood stylus inscribe illegible Greek letters on wet beach sand—
     washed away at high tide by Poseidon's mighty hand?

Silly, defiant son of Daedalus!

Did he glance skyward and see his unnamed Mother
     in the smirking Sun that receded past his greedy reach—a green coin?

Icarus Suicide

Did Icarus mean to fall
and drown in the Aegean Sea
when he reached that zenith
point?   Eyes

on the green prize for skyward impulse—
surely, suicide was not
his bling thing—even if the sun was
the glitter gun that stapled him into dog-
eared mythology books, and
all the other bookmarked
places of art history, burning
like Savonarola
acolytes.   Icarus,

the darling,
slipshod thing—fallen from blazing
latitudes, winged merboy, new hybrid
creature, uroboric signifier—floating,
twisting, contorting into an
ampersand (salt-
speckled pretzel &)

forever added onto, a
waxy dust mote in the blinking
eye, shapeshifting—scrawny
fetus fossil; suicide a
retrospective conjecture underpinning the pinwheeling
pinioned kingpin boy to justify
his bad splash.

Icarus | Epicanthus

Icarus | Epicanthus

Black hair filament
hovering before my right eye—
DNA strand twisting a
tangled tango; blink, and un-
lock that algorithmic
dance; blink again, and chase
away that pesky black speck—
like burnt Icarus drifting,
hanging on the epicanthic edge
of my eyelid; shifting vitreous
floater.

Moon Palace King

He shrivels into mummy-
sized coffin dimensions, like a
secretly decaying tooth
in the mouth of Time—festering into
the moon's halitosis, porous and
respectable, sporting Prufrock's
askew neckties—unraveling in
the heavy direction that gravity loves. We

never had a strong common language,
despite the black hair and high cheekbones
we share genetically—just the child's
Japanese tripping off my stuttering

tongue. I'd never understood
his need for three consecutive wives
(anachronistic exorbitance)—Mother being
sloppy seconds to the unknown
first, angelically dead. Third wife's
deal was the worst of all—she'd felt
coerced to kiss the behind of some leering devil
that winked at her in a moth-eaten universe. Today,

Father is the gold-toothed mummy—
Don Giovanni of amorphous days
in New York City, king of Moon Palace restaurant
on Broadway & West 112th Street near
Columbia University, where all the Beat Generation
guys did their beatific thing equally sloppily;
and the pink crocuses bloomed each spring
on sidewalk islands; and the grey-
haired shopping bag lady howled beneath
the painted building façade reading:

"The wages of sin is death
But the gift of God
Is eternal life
In Jesus Christ, Our Lord."

Father was also the Taiwanese Malcolm X
whose family name was an overused signifier
in the buzzing silence wake of slammed-
down phone receivers on crackling,
cacophonous death threats for supporting Taiwan
during the Nixon years. He was

the lean, sinewy man in the white
wife beater shirt,

who flung open
the window sash to yell,
"*Bakayarō!*"
at upstairs neighbors pounding piano
keys in the humid New York City night;

who playfully struck the back of
my head when I'd switched on the fixtured ceiling lights in
my Burgess Hall bedroom
in glaring daylight hours;

who yelled at me, Mother, and Mei-Mei
for Charmin toilet paper overuse (when a taut, blackened
public rope had served that function for him
in rural Tainan);

who instructed me and Mei-Mei to repeat
after him, "*Zhōnghuá mínguó wànsuì!*"
and wave our little ROC flags;

who embarrassed me by speaking broken
English to my American playmates;

whose long lean hand spooned syrupy apricot mush into the
open giggling mouth of my baby sister;

Moon Palace King reigning supreme over
all those steaming Chinese dishes, the gaping fish being
the spicy spectacle, freeze-framed on the largest
platter. His

energy spilled beyond
the restaurant into our Burgess Hall living
room, where he talked for hours without end with friends, colleagues, whomever he'd
        roped into his mesmerized circle—till Mother appeared like a sleepy ghost in her

Woolworth's nightgown to heat up our blackened wok
in our kitchenette till the oily sizzle woke her up,
and his talk crackled into incomprehensible jokes—flash in the pan
in the dark of night.

NYC childhood memories of undivorced Father remain—
vaguely colored streamers from the heart's broken
piñata—bandages unraveling from the mummified feet of Time.

Shikata ga Nai (Let It Be)

Stoic acceptance

      - not passive acquiescence
      - not dumb cattle herded into packed boxcars
      - not subservient Japs (as

           though truncation diminishes self-esteem)—

swallowing the bitter spittle
of outrage re. E.O. 9066
like green tea without the usual
ceremony.   Heavy steps,

        overstuffed duffel bags—

all that two arms can carry
(all that the heart can carry)

Shikata ga nai.   Swallow, lunge   forward
gravel   crunch [toxic *gaman*]

overblown chrysanthemum heads drop
           with the weight of

apology [*mōshi wake nai*] for being

Japanese Americans at the wrong time (as
  though there were a right time for these   porous   hybrid
                            many-petaled things)—
The skies above Manzanar were sheets of motheaten kimono silk—
    taut with anxiety, mottled with unanswered questions, pinpricked with
cruel stars;

The lacquered *bento* boxes
The *sake* cups
The porcelain rice bowls
The spoons, the chopsticks,
    the *obi* sashes matchless with lost kimono   pieces   and the children
        without their *Hinamatsuri* dolls (where are they now?)

Cucumbers and   plums pickle in formaldehyde   jars

Shikata ga nai.

Hiroshima & Nagasaki

The flash

The crash

The ash.

Decimation was instantaneous—skeletons etched upon asphalt,

        shadows sick with radiation

            vomited skyward curses—

The True Man hanging from the over-blossoming

tree of public panic   unlynched.

Gas Panic

Inhaling the same toxic air—
                    ominous shift of carbon molecules
in Hibiya line subway cars—morning
commuters held in
            the nausea (gag reflex)

ignoring beckoning silk Hanae Mori
handkerchiefs; contact lenses shriveling
            like oversized fish scales in reddening eyes;
manicured fingertips fluttering toward disheveling
                        hair—cell phones sinking in deep pockets—

briefcases dropping—soft sleepy slump of
bodies ["*Tasukete kudasai!*" unstated,
"*Iie, daijōbu desu,*" contending]—nylon ladders stretching down
                        panty-hosed legs—high heels breaking
into staccato runs—toward diminuendo of public trust—

allegedly, first responders are never
bystanders in Tokyo, and Japanese commuters are
perfect bioterrorism victims; both apathy and courtesy are
paralyzing: How can tacitly implicit privacy barriers be

penetrated without shattering plexiglass selves into a million
carbon molecules? After all, self-

truncation in Japan is like an amputated
yakuza pinky, literal *yubi-kiri*,
kamikaze self-sacrifice to Shinto gods—blood pact,
and childhood promise of a thousand needles swallowed—
                                      a crinkling shrinkage of cringing selves,
giftwrapped in polyester *furoshiki*. The corporate gift

of permanent service to the *kaisha* had unraveled that volatile morning of
umbrella-point-punctured liquid sarin sacks—devotion to Aum Shinrikyō
being a toxic alternative—

and after Shōko Asahara's execution, he bloated into the *yubi-kiri* pinky,
amputated public promise.

The Doll

Saddled with a doll,
hard, slippery, oversized, celluloid thing—
no purpose for it, besides staring,
equally wide-eyed, into its blinking
eyes, fringed with black
plastic eyelashes.

Celluloid weight,
aircraft encumbrance—shoved into the overhead
bin, replica of the hollow girl-child
I was, shoveling strawberry ice cream into
my cold mouth
with a tiny wood spoon
  at Haneda Airport. Then, the nauseating descent toward JFK International—

a pillow on my churning tummy
filling loose seatbelt space, making up for
  the airborne difference. Surely, the doll was rolling around, vomiting
turbulence—

till the aircraft landed, a serene
  origami crane gliding across creamy runways in the cold
        strawberry-colored dawn.

Duck, Duck, Goose

Round and round, the boys they ran—
around the circle of girls in demure pigtails,
and tight braids—impatient to be goosed,
to receive the golden egg, prize without King
Midas' compromising touch. The
boys skirted the issue—attempting to tag each
other outside the squirming circle of
bored girls, nurturing goose eggs—pulling each
other's pigtails, laughing, squealing, knowing
there never would be a breach in their golden circle—
an endless game with no winner—
just the constipated goose.

"Wanted"

That smiling brunette, so
unlike a mugshot;
the camera was her friend—
its flash carving out for her a
haloed whitespace.

"WANTED: Patricia Campbell Hearst,"
read the 1974 B/W poster at the
Amsterdam Ave. P.O. near
Columbia University, the decade
when I'd learned to read, a gawking
uniformed first-grader at
St. Hilda's & St. Hugh's School. Patty

Hearst morphed into my RTS symptom
after 2001 till I felt like a badass
white woman, my head a scrambled egg,
imagining a mannequin wielding a
machine gun—ripping up tawdry
marquees with scathing gunfire—
tortuous machinations contorting torsos into askew
positions—feeding stale bread crumbs
to the vulturous media. Over the years,

my scrambled head coalesced, bloomed,
a gold chrysanthemum—and the SLA
symbol wriggled into its proper archived place—
a castrated 7-headed cobra.

Girl Bathing

Thrust of puny
pelvis beneath
running bathtub faucet—
washaway the viscous
stigma of odor;
strange, pink parts
of me clean &
quivering;
thudding cataract of
bathwater, silky
absolution—

till the Gorgon
roar of a distant
gorge (untied
Gordian knot
of pink entrails)—
and swoon of
black asterisks
recalled the endless
Coney Island
rollercoaster
descent—

scrawny, sallow
buttocks hit
white bathtub floor—
dirty gurgle of
water down the
gargoyle drain;
curdling
fear of
the blackout
that didn't
happen.

Empire State Building Soup

Hot water spurt—
scalding cataract, hiss
of disappointment—
into the void of
the metallic place
where the paper
cup should have
dropped. I

gaped at the steam,
the yellowish
inane water for
chicken soup gurgling
down the pipeline
of a malfunctioning
vending machine
on the observation
deck of the Empire State
Building, over-
looking the silvery
panorama of yellow
taxicabs crawling

along W. 34th
St., over-diligent ants I
wanted to smash
like the undropped
soup cup.

TV Dinner

Snowbound nights when my PhD-seeking mom
decided to give herself a break; and me,
and Mei-Mei a treat, I relished
each steaming Swanson TV dinner item, nestled
in crinkled aluminum foil, an American *bento* box:

Veal parmigiana meatloaf
      smothered in tomato sauce and cheese;
Mashed potatoes,
     fluffy white and buttery yellow;
Green peas,
     ultimate food for kids
to play with;

    Apple strudel,
   central dessert delight,
    ensconced in tiniest
aluminum square,
beckoning
    baked jewel, apple of
     my hungry eye.

Nothing compared to Mom's
oven-baked Scotch eggs, of
course, but those TV

dinners enabled me and my baby
sister to see
who could stick

a
pea
on
every
fork
prong

first.

Channel Surfers

Round and round the Japanese
TV frames flashed by—midsong
commercials—decapitated talking
heads—a whizzing jar of Shiseido
night cream in an amputated
hand—zap! long-haired screaming girl
running from a lumbering Texas chainsaw-
wielding... zap! into psychedelic

Russian roulette repeat of commercial
chants; decapitated heads; amputated
hands—girl still screaming and
running—hair darkly plastered down
the skull of her head—abjected
spectacle fragments of ambivalent
voyeurism, for me and my kid sister—
compulsive channel surfers, our screams over-
lapping with the girl's—wanting to
unplug, dump that TV into the murky
Sumida River oozing diarrheically—
beyond the bedroom terrace—after one
more round—just one more glimpse...
zap!

Grandmother's Kitchen

That dark unlit space,
a haven for my grandmother,
shuffling, groping
around for some odd,
forgotten thing—nothing
as handy, or American,
as Tupperware, nor
as concrete as that one
missing chopstick, but
necessary, nonetheless. Yet,

she'd managed
to pickle *oshinko* cucumbers
and eggplants, the *nuka-miso* stench
being her friend—to emerge from that dark,
unlikely space with a plate of ground beef omelet—
a miracle, considering her aversion to butter—
"*Bata-kusai*," she'd mutter
about anything "Western" (I suppose my
white *gaijin* boyfriends reeked
of butter, too, like overfed geese). That

kitchen had been
her inviolate space that Banana
Yoshimoto would've praised to the white-
tiled skies (had it been visible)—*nuka-miso* reek
and incense fragrance intermingling in a pungent
vapory dance throughout that ramshackle two-
storied house in *Suna-machi* till my

mother modernized Grandmother's kitchen: she
flooded electric lights into it—plastered mildewed wood walls with pink rose vinyl wallpaper—
crammed the latest refrigerator model with meat and dairy products [blocks of *Yuki-Jirushi* butter] for
me and Mei-Mei, who'd grown into a long-legged American teenager in the porous City of Sand.

Since that kitchen makeover,
Grandmother would appear before us (while
we watched Madonna writhing
like a fallen snake goddess on MTV), kimono-less, muttering to herself,
her flattened-out, shriveled-up breasts exposed—
a grey specter we ignored. But, Mother
said *Obaa-chan* loved the new microwave
that steamed leftover rice to perfect white fluff.

Lunch Hour

Wordless, the Japanese businessmen
accepted from me the lacquered bento boxes
and steaming bowls of miso soup I
placed before them.   We gazed upon
red silky maguro slices; tempura shrimp
tails peeking beyond coats of crisply bubbled
batter; teriyaki-glazed tender
chicken pieces; green dollop of
wasabi; pale pink petals of shaved
ginger, each flavor
compartmentalized.   Solemn umami moment

during blur of lunch hour rush at Suibi—
I bowed, turned, and two white businessmen,
who had already been served, winked
at me, and said, "We'd like some
attention." I

blinked at them, and Icarus was a   speck   of

green seaweed on the edge of my
fluttering eyelid.

Japanese Idols

The building roof was not high enough for their
descent toward the simple
place they'd always wanted
to inhabit.

Harajuku
strawberry ice cream,
chocolate crepes
and Hello Kitty key chains
were all they'd ever wanted
like other Japanese teenage girls;

not the overwork,
the unspoken harassment
the PMS cramps
the obligatory smiling faces they'd
shown to the public before emojis emerged into iPhones.

What Yasuko Endō &
Yukiko Okada had really wanted was
the freedom to fly sunward
without crashing &
dying—kamikaze Icarus girls,
their cremated ash drifting upon godwind.

Say Her Asian Name

Since her arrival in the United States of America,
her Chinese name (whatever it had
been) blurred away—a smudged sequence of ink-
                    brushed ideographs,
signifying sounds butchered by tripping, Anglicizing
tongues, lopped into bite-
sized *ching-chong* onomatopoeia,
off-key singsong syllables (two

Zen hands clapping). She was
the Atlanta gunman's pathological
symptom, his sin,

his massage parlor whore,
his Orientalized desire victim,
his paper China doll tucked

away into stale fortune cookies
incinerated after the spark of
candlelight vigils
in March 2021 ignited #StopAsianHate
hashtags, and her papery

edges caught fire—the Asian
American dream gunned
down (no mountains of gold)—Chinatowns
                  oozing away—eliding glossy tourist pamphlets,
sticky with chop suey fingerprints.
Even now, she has no real (Chinese) name

(Maxine Hong Kingston's "no-
name woman"), the spectral signifier rising from

phoenix ash. So, say her Asian name (her no-name
woman's name): Xiaojie ("Emily") Tan,

"*Xiaojie*," a Mandarin prefix, and slang
for "prostitute"; "Emily," a whitewashing
(parenthetical) afterthought—she is the ideograph slipping away
toward the lexicography of new hashtags—
that smudgy marginal gloss—that drop of coagulated vigil candlewax;
paper money burning for the unappeasable gods
squatting on gold mountains.

Bachelor Party

He glanced upward at
the dancer, his wallet bulging
singles.   The writhing white body on the Fancy
Pants Club stage was

the incorrect
object of his gaze
for which he was
bludgeoned by a
baseball bat, mistaken for Japanese—
when the rising yen, and the influx of Toyotas and Hondas and Subarus threatened to
    usurp automotive factory jobs in Detroit, Michigan, a wilderness of spare parts, rusting.

So much for a bachelor party,
where tinsel, sequins, and feathers whirled away—
    and bartenders ignored the greasy dollars, quarters, dimes, and nickels on sticky
    countertops, and the untouched shot glasses brimming kamikazes.

The baseball bat
that killed Vincent Chin struck a homerun toward heaven—
    leaving behind on the baseball-sized earth #StopAsianHate hashtags decades too late.

Stereotype

Lisa eats her evening meal
with chopsticks, bird's eye
view from my patio. She

could've been
the Chinese Lady
on voyeuristic display
in 1834. I see her

historicized vulnerability through white
venetian blinds, her Chinese name
uninscribed on the blank
label of her askew
mailbox. She

radically modifies the quiet
China doll stereotype, as I hear her
raucous laughter at late night hours
through YouTube jazz blasting through my earphones—
her antics normalized, no

choppy ching-chong syllables,
nor chopsticks stuck in piled-high

black hair, nor slanty
almond eyes, nor bound feet.   Just

the loud American voice, the girlish
shriek, the fluffy white cat
in her stout cradling arms, clueless.

Umami

Essential component,
      a challenge to capture like slippery eel,
            yet to be broiled in soy sauce, sugar, and *mirin*
(think *unagi*). Umami,

the balance of all five flavors, countable on one hand:
sweet, salty, bitter, sour, spicy—
blending into one lovely flavor with the opening of buds—
the ripening of seasons—the precarious

balancing act—slippery
      acrobatics across the thick porous tongue.

Icarus Redux

Icarus Redux

Green roses bloomed for Icarus
beneath his pasty heels
when they hit the Aegean seawaves
with a vociferous splash.

He morphed into the flipped
bird at high noon when he gave the finger
to the sun god Helios—falling out of the burning sky—a charred piece
    of debris, floating like a dust mote, or

a waxy   speck   in the blinking

eye.

His ego waxed as the sun waxed shedding
hot golden tears—feathers sadly drifting from the cunningly wrought osier
framework of synthetic wings—upon the oily surface of the sea, an interminable
canvas of sloppy   experiments, choppy with roiling acrylic paint.

He then became a work of art (however
crappily executed)—gawked at in museum galleries,
featured in poems by W. H. Auden and William Carlos Williams (albeit

to illustrate such things as the massive indifference of teeming human life—
busy as geeky ants, and almost as blind).

He even stood in for suicide Sylvia
and all the other heroic icons who failed
to die the normal geriatric way.

So, when green roses bloomed for Icarus,
green became the iconic color *par excellence*; oxidized copper pennies
became the tarnished currency—circulating corrosive envy and burning bile—
and Icarus was minted in accolades of green.

What mortician of high noon can reverse this process of oxidization, restore
the clean gold face of the sun, the wings of our Copernican darling—
accomplish the mission of Daedalus without unseemly detriment?

Green roses bloomed for all of us
when Icarus fell

from the

sky.

Cheese Icarus

Peripheral
paraphernalia burned
away, Icarus is
the cheese
that stands
alone,
porous like
Swiss,
greening like
gorgonzola—
sun-grilled,
sandwiched
between
sky & sea,
melting into tailless
tuna in the oily
Aegean.

M.C. Escher
convergence of
fish & bird,
Icarus is
also a mosaic

piece, a
nursery rhyme
fragment, cast-
away fingernail
paring; a floating
obscene
signifier—
but always,
the solitary
cheese; single
waxy Kraft
slice, residue
of manufactured
American
hunger, standing
alone.

Dumpster Diving

Surplus of America,
debris of the Indiana University Bloomington
academic year 2014–2015
piled up high in the overflowing
dumpster at 417 S. Fess next door—
emitting stench of raw meat,
black buzz of flies like animate
watermelon seeds; buzzards

create havoc in their usual
pecking order—shadows diving
in and out, round each sharp,
rusty, curious corner—

flickering flashlights. Wet mass of melting
frozen fruit packages from Kroger—
blackberry juice oozing diluted purple
stain, like blurry hieroglyphics
inscribed in the blood of gods, disowned
and yet devoured. The

stench, the ooze, the compulsion, the shame—
the socioeconomically equalizing act of dumpster

diving makes us vultures
devouring the same carrion with varying gradations of
gratuitous grace.

Diva

Swift stardom
Millennial | Gen. Z icon
sequined and bejeweled
cubic zirconia flash
across exorbitant stages—
captured on Instagram,
TikTok, Spotify, Apple Music,
YouTube; woke, smokey-eyed diva,
more pliant than plastic
Barbie, and less pink
and compliant, moving to the correct
choreography of narrow
hips canceling Shakira,
shaking overstuffed moneybags—
shedding snakeskin & green
pennies—striptease for a new
breed of voyeurs.   Swift haters

do their blingless thing, shaking grey
heads, wannabe millennial
billionaires without the inconvenience
of being hated, too, or
vulnerable like Icarus

falling, a squawking
chicken—plucked feathers floating
on the oily surface of the Aegean Sea
like tailored sequins.

After the Fire

Before the fire next door
at Rara Avis Apartments on 417 S. Fess,
the dumpster had over-

flowed richly, a stinky marketplace,
inviting tenants to fling
overstuffed black trash bags from
the windows above. The American

flag serving as a shade
at a glowing window
bothered me some, but

it became all right
after the fire—flames that ravaged
the second-floor corner
apartments, facing away
from the dumpster—blackened into
eye-sockets in the skull of the building. Today,

the Rara Avis dumpster has been
normalized by bona fide trash:

- flattened-out, stained, frozen food cartons
- storm-broken tree branches
- yawning styrofoam clamshell carry-out food boxes
- soggy cylindrical toilet paper cores
- battered, dented, venetian window blinds
- plastic buckets of scum-saturated sponges
  and half-used Clorox cleaner bottles

scavengers discouraged like overfed
vultures.

The Neighborhood Cat

Crawling along the shrubbery fringe,
      the cat came bounding, meowing up
           the twelve rust-flecked patio steps of
our multiplex house—at Srijita's beckoning. She

named him "Sir Christopher Robin," and sprinkled Meow Mix into recyclable
           plastic bowls on the baking cement floor of our shared patio,
while I poured half-and-half onto a thick saucer,
           watching with satisfaction, as our adopted outdoor cat
devoured the multi-colored fish-shaped crackers, and lapped up
      the milky liquid before it curdled beneath
the July sun. He was

our delightful darling till Srijita's shriek alerted me to his farewell
gift planted on our patio: a dead baby rabbit. I

last glimpsed him ambling away toward the
           CAT backhoe loader in the nearby alley—
beyond which he vanished   into August's sepia dusk.

Wife

The wife,
suburban
life-
   style goddess,
Wi-Fi fife
shrilling beastly
beatitude, harpy
outlined with a
pink Sharpie
   —shedding feathers &
sequins
   sequentially—tamed
shrew,

burnt Hestia
aged Helen (dangling
frayed

apron strings)

shriveled Eve,
pared Granny
Smith apple

slices, folded into black-
    bird pies, cookie
cutter wife,
    hungering for
serpent
    seed.

Bikini Body

Every body is a "bikini body"
if there's a bikini on it.
That's the consoling definition
    rigged on the skeleton of the bodhi tree—
dropping overripe fruit.   The

body, an
anorexic commodity of bulimic fasting
vomiting nutrients—

or, a mesomorphic prize
of exorbitant gym memberships;

or, a flabby letdown
    bloating from unused weights and treadmills,
potato chip crumbs accumulating in sofa crevices with greening pennies.

Anatomy of a bikini:
Triangular polyester pieces
    stitched together by factory laborers in China,
intended to conceal (yet paradoxically)
    highlight boobs and asses and pubic regions (unholy Trinity,
Bermuda Triangle of stringy stringency)

- Raquel Welch
- Kate Upton
- Kim K.

Bikini overkill
(courtesy of Google Images,
accessed while drunk on Bud Light 6-packs).

Iconized sex goddess caryatids
carrying the weight of impossible standards,
ossified into celluloid Barbies—
crumbling into dust and pixels. So,

every body can wear a bikini—
        flipped bird feathers float, mingling with crumbled
caryatid dust motes,
        and Icarus performs a burlesque somersault beneath the laughing
sun.

The Date (August 7, 1930)

She tweaked the bow
in her dirty blonde hair—rolling red lipstick over smiling lips
that puckered into a practice kiss before her vanity
mirror. Her dream

guy had asked her out on a date. (But,
why was her silvery reflection rippling
                 away beyond the blink of her yearning blue eyes?)

No matter, because her deviled eggs were perfect, her
picnic basket, so very pretty!　　Yet,

she wondered if her bow would remain
straight, if her lip
color would smudge, fade, flake off—

She planted a red kiss upon the mirror's slippery,
mercurial surface.

Clutching the picnic basket, she
ran toward the Marion County courthouse square,
breathless.

Sweating, unwashed bodies pressed against her
on all four sides—(where is he?)   her bow askew again. She
slipped a deviled egg into her
mouth—mayonnaise oozing delight.

Fluffy white-bread sandwiches, delectable,
cucumber slices cooling her tongue—each picnic basket item
vanishing with a smiling, stifled

burp. Then, the roar through Eustachian corridors—
the basket lost in the trample of feet.   Vultures screeched across the Indiana horizon

as she glanced upward
at the two black bodies swinging from the tree—
forbidden fruit in August heat.   She

vomited, as the sun receded into a
black dot

and she collapsed into the roaring stampede.

Shrove Tuesday

All the lawns on Mentone Avenue are mowed on Wednesdays.
To do so on any other day, was inconceivable (a

sacrilege). So, she would wait, as usual, till the following

Wednesday, despite the encumbrance of inconvenient
calendar days.   She laid

down her shears, perspiring, after clipping
off the heads of overblown
                    wild roses, grass growing above her itchy ankles.

What day was it? She gazed through sprinkler mist down the length of Mentone Avenue—the
                    neat little houses with their green square patches of lawn—unshuttered windows like
the sockets of skulls, watching her.   Aphids

crawling among the browning white rose petals bothered her—
                    more so, the thickening, unkempt, withering grass.

Shouldn't she level the green line of her lawn to match her neighbors' down that beautifully
                    uniform sunlit stretch on Mentone Avenue?   So, today must be

Wednesday.

Why, every day is Wednesday!

Wild weeding days winding through all the lovely encroaching wilderness.   Her
              lawn mower buzzed, a ravenous buzzard—fragrance of freshly cut
              grass mingling with the stink of beheaded roses, already compost.

She felt the lawn mower's rattle in her throat,
the noonday sun, a receding black dot,

              and she suddenly remembered—it was Shrove Tuesday.

Thanksgiving 2003

Wade through panoramic
multiplex—thickly
cinematic in XL wool
underwear &
slick outerwear
(treacherous
circumnavigation).

Disheveled mothers
bulge sweatshirts &
Victoria's Secret pantylines

(drip secrets from your
steamy gravy pans &
Martha
Stewart ovens).

Plastic ice cream spoons
break off the 25% fat
rate of DVD camcorders—sprint an oscillating test
run around baby limbs & untucked
shirts over toddler
tummies—sprawling family-sized

fast food picnics in makeshift
corners of your local mall

(Little Jack Horner is
horny tonight & homeless in our secure Homeland).

Rush & raid dwindling
merchandise stock while
equal opportunities skyrocket to zenith
splurge of belch & cardiac
tourniquet constrict a tight
elastic circulation of

commodity prices reaching beyond lifeless livestock eyes grazing Indiana
grassland & blazing sunset horizon—uprooted promises soaking up
midnight dishwater.

So, let's stimulate the war economy with killer
Wal-Mart deals while the president grins in the mess halls of Baghdad
festooned with orange crepe streamers & papier-mâché turkeys & rousing
roustabout cheers for the vainglory of the United States of America.

All hail to the president of America who flew on a clandestine iconoclastic
        rabble-rousing ball-busting mission into the desiccated (and
        desecrated) desert areas of the occupied.

All hail to the president's men who dispatched the dude with circumspect
        precision like a precariously gift-wrapped Playboy bunny jumping
        out of a dynamo dream cake with rapid stun gun loinfire.

All hail to the armed forces of America who ignited a long & messy camel
        trot toward Iron Hammered emancipation of falling

Viagara-powered suicidal limbs firing a vasectomy of blanks into a
        gallstone hailstorm, prefabricating applause & ironing out
Faberge mirage curtains.

Last Supper in Terre Haute

The sky was a leaden slab oppressing the horizontal land beneath it;
      nimbus clouds the color of jail suit orange collided and coalesced

      like dirty cotton candy rolling into the unkempt backyards of
      Bloomington, Indiana the morning Timothy McVeigh was
      scheduled to die in Terre Haute.

Iconically speaking, he was a lethal injection in the promethean heartland
      of America, wielding a poisonous pen that resurrected "Invictus"
      in the cold refrigerator dawn, eliciting an extreme aversion for
      chocolate mint ice cream, the last supper

      doled out on the long spoon of public concession—spanning the
      distance between himself and the collateral damage at the Alfred
      P. Murrah Federal Building in Oklahoma City.

After the execution, he morphed into a dirty animus incubus coalescing
      viscously like toxic orange storm clouds—the diarrheic Indiana
      skies

vomiting pints of chocolate mint ice cream laced with sodium pentothal,
pancuronium bromide and potassium chloride—circulating intravenously
throughout the sepia-colored landscapes of the United States of America.

Gunshot

The only difference is
the direction of the gunpoint. When

lines blur between self and other, the difference becomes
dangerous—unlike tidy dichotomies

we ingest like pellets of dopamine. Either
way, it's the same uroboros gagging on both tail ends
of the same grey spectrum.

Archived Realia in Littleton, Colorado

Columbines have bloomed again
     in Littleton, Colorado, since the 1999 high school shootings. Their

sadly drooping golden
     heads acknowledge the sweet April shoot through adamant roots.
                  The high school library was

a gunnery field of overwrought
          machinations and decimated
obligations, a sanctuary
     desecrated by gunfire—Dewey Decimal numbers oozing
               off monographic Mylar spines
[inveterate vertebrae]

till yellow evidence cards begged autopsies
among sadly blooming
columbines,
   and the apocalyptic
       realia was, duly counted, collected, collated, and

cataloged—a weeping archive.

Last Lunch in Littleton, Colorado

Flap of vulture wings,
unheard, till the black
speck in the corner of
            her eye waxed into the
strange sun—too gold.   Was

her last lunch a
white bread sandwich?

- Ham & Cheese
- Egg salad
- PBJ
- Tuna fish

Or, bagel halves smeared with Philadelphia
cream cheese?   A pack of Lays potato chips
tossed into her brown paper bag (an
afterthought), or

- Carrot sticks
- Pickle spears
- Apple slices
- 2 chocolate chip cookies

- Fig newtons
- Skittles
- Olives
- Babybel cheeses

Why stare into her brown paper bag tunnelling through her pink esophagus (sarcophagus) into
the vulture eye of the noonday sun—a receding black dot?

The last lunch of Rachel Scott
is one of many unanswered
questions, as vulture wings beat—
and the wayward wind filled her brown paper lunch bag, standing in for her

pretty Promethean heart.

American Pietà

She glanced down
at the bloated, disfigured face
of her beautiful son;

American Pietà.   His
whistling breath
stirred unwanted
embers—sparks that lodged within the
                desiccated beams of the intricate scaffolding of Southern rural racism in Drew,
Mississippi, 28 August 1955.

She'd wanted
the most solid, gold things for him,

not the media vultures preying upon the preserved corpse, abject spectacle,
             silent testimony for the world to look upon—elephant in the room, bleached in camera flash.

The Iconization of Rosa Parks

When they tucked her away in a bed
of roses in the Capitol Rotunda,
did the Republican thorns
scrape away her dignity
the color of red sea
ignominy—scratch out
eyes that no longer saw
a divided America?

When she refused to rise from her sticky
seat, did she think she would be
queen of the Civil Rights movement
in the humiliating carbon monoxide
stench that clung to her
heavy askew skirt,
seamstress stitching together the
arbitrarily missing pieces of our divided,
wounded, gunshot America and her long-armed
sons tilling the earth for the good salt
beneath the soiled bedrock
and her large-breasted daughters
bending their heads to the blowing storm?

She rises now from her seat
of ignominy in terribly
scarlet glory—into the historical ether,
to the graffiti of noise
behind tombstone
eyelids—an articulate icon
that never spoke,
nor raised a dark fist
against the adamant storm clouds.

She is the ironic democracy
silent iconoclast
superintendent of dreams
attended by servile roses.

Ferguson, Missouri
(August 2014)

Beauty Town was back in business
At least for a while in Ferguson, Missouri

Where at least 4 other beauty supply stores were vandalized
Where Michael Brown was fatally gunned down
Where Darren Wilson was not indicted

Where James Knowles III ran unopposed for mayor in 2014
Where an estimated 94% of law enforcement officers are white
Where African Americans comprise 67.4% of the city's population
   according to the 2010 census

Where approximately a quarter of the residents live below the federal poverty line

Where Scott Olson got arrested for shooting protest photos for Getty Images
Where demonstrators got tear-gassed by police in riot gear
Where 40+ businesses were looted or vandalized or incinerated
   according to Twitter #hashtags

Where beauty was destroyed and resurrected again and again
Where the Black Lives Matter movement started up and galvanized the nation.

Beauty Town was back in business
At least for a while in Ferguson, Missouri.

COVID America

It began with the "Chinese virus"—injected invective into mainstream
        media flows—no filters—till the United States of America became

a filthy petri dish—breeding, incubating resurrected #hashtags and
multiple trun-
cations, shutdowns, lockdowns, one-

handed masturbation sessions—Walmart shopping sprees for toilet paper and hand sanitizer—as
though 6 feet apart weren't long enough distance between Democrats and Republicans—the length of
an average-sized coffin in America. And now,

masked faces are politically correct emojis, and schoolchildren and
teachers are collateral damage, waiting to be counted and collected—
slipping through the cracks of the
2020 census,

while Karen became the princess ensconced in ice at the glassy apex of Capitol Hill, and George Floyd
became the summer #hashtag excuse erupting from claustrophobic suburban closets. If the coronavirus
is a

left-wing government hoax, then, the KKK is a masquerade of
sadomasochistic Blacks, smirking in white hoods.

Halt TikTok negotiations because no American's got a "chinaman's chance."
Swallow bleach to sanitize mansions of the mind inundated with misinformation—
Pimp Polaroids for Facebook Likes and Twitter followers—
Keep digging in the gold mines of overflowing
    dumpsters with rubber gloves—pick out soggy Cheerios with OCD childhood spoons (because all
lives matter in Heaven & Hell).

A COVID test is like a Shirley Jackson lottery, but the black dot is the cue ball shot across vast green
fields where stripes and solids, and life and death, are equal opportunities [for all].

America, the big-boobed nation, is not particularly interested in flattening out curves—because
bigger is better, and Biggest is Best. So, let's go ahead, and say that COVID-19 is symptomatic of the
American diseases of:

- racism (and all other 'isms and orgasmic schisms)
- corporate greed
- homelessness
- obesity

sugar, salt, butter, cheese, red meat, fast food, barbecue sauce overkill—
Mrs. Butterworth, Uncle Ben & Aunt Jemima, the ménage-à-trois falling
off their respective supermarket shelves like shot-down Confederate statues. And BLM is

the graffiti scrawl
of underground discourses like the N-word, the F-word, the word branded upon the obscene, obese

flesh of the (denying, white) American brain; the Word with which the world began (and could end).
So,

cover up the Big American Motor Mouth (speak no evil)—
spitting out epithelial epithets—using leftover duct tape from 9-11 terror alert days;

Fauci & Kevorkian morph into siamese twins in paranoid collective consciousness—
in a nation ruled by old white men.

When will Uncle Sam wear a dress? (when he/she/they are dressed to kill?)
When will we cry uncle?
When will Mother know best?
When will entropic atoms coalesce into utopia?

Nobody in America wants to wear a mask
that covers up full, luscious, smiling lips (Cover Girl disenfranchised).

Nobody wants to comply
with government mandates in a democratic America—a gag bag of party
tricks; a piñata exploding plastic Cracker Jack prizes in your face.

America is an immigrant's wet dream—
the green residue of pinched pennies.

America is a melting pot of
incompatible condiments—a conundrum of pundits;

lamb stew of Crab Rangoons and national lampoons; Willy Wonka's chocolatier wok,
and Charlie Chan's ChapStick factory—

enigmatic reduction of USPS operations—
generates nostalgia for the taste of glue on the sticky back-
sides of US postage stamps.

America is a silly thing,
America is a bleached-blonde virago.
"America" is a floating signifier—
Hollywood's mega-mouth "sound & fury."

America is a masquerade of giggling, scrawny, pimpled, dimpled teenagers.
America is a narcissist, reflected in gilt-edged, gargantuan, baroque mirrors—guilt-tripping down strip
malls—stripped of all shame, like the naked Emperor.

American dads curse at barbecue grills that won't start up;
American moms upbraid their pigtailed daughters for smashing their overstuffed piggy banks
prematurely—
American kids vie for the biggest unbroken cookie;
American dogs sniff the biggest crotches.

And it all ends with the "Chinese virus"—eating its own grey spermatozoic rat-tail uroborically—
gagging on the dust of desecrated Edens—shriveled mummy Chinatowns scattered across the pock-
marked moon face of America; the Polaroid cheese that stands
alone on one shriveled Zen leg.

Icarus Obverse

If Icarus were minted on a greening penny, its
obverse would be a flipped bird—
Icarus sprouting fragile wings from sloping
shoulder blades, shivering beneath the sun's hot
scrutiny. Icarus giving the finger to his father &
to the sun god Helios. Icarus was that finger
itself, stroking the raggedy edge of the Aegean sea waves—
planting accolades in unlikely
places. The other side

of the flipped coin is always greener
than its coppery obverse; Icarus burning.

Author of one full-length poetry collection and four poetry chapbooks, Hiromi Yoshida is a finalist for the New Women's Voices Poetry Prize, and a semifinalist for the Gerald Cable Book Award. While serving as a poetry reader for *Flying Island Journal,* and as secretary of the Writers Guild at Bloomington, she coordinates the Guild's Last Sunday Poetry reading series.

ALSO AVAILABLE

Icarus Superstar (2023)

Icarus Redux (2021)

Epicanthus (2021)

Icarus Burning (2020)

LITERARY CRITICISM

"Joyce & Jung: The Four Stages of Eroticism" in *A Portrait of the Artist as a Young Man,* second edition (2022)

MORE ROADSIDE PRESS TITLES:

Bar Guide for the Seriously Deranged
Alan Catlin

Born on Good Friday
Nathan Graziano

Under Normal Conditions
Karl Koweski

The Dead and the Desperate
Dan Denton

Clown Gravy
Misti Rainwater-Lites

Walking Away
Michael D. Grover

All in a Pretty Little Row
Dan Provost

These Are the People in Your Neighbourhood
Jordan Trethewey

They Said I Wasn't College Material
Scot Young

Radio Water
Francine Witte

And Blackberries Grew Wild
Susan Mickelberry

Licorice Heart
Miles Budimir

MORE ROADSIDE PRESS TITLES:

Disposable Darlings
Todd Cirillo

Full Moon Midnight
Belinda Subraman

Innocent Postcards
John Pietaro

Cistern Latitudes
James Duncan

Another Saturday Night in Jukebox Hell
Alan Catlin

Abandoned By All Things
Karl Koweski

Ain't These Sorrows Sweet?
Lauren Scharhag

Gregory Corso: Ten Times a Poet
Leon Horton, Editor

She Throws Herself Forward to Stop the Fall
Dave Newman

We Don't Get to Write the Ending
Aleathia Drehmer

These Many Cold Winters of the Heart
Ryan Quinn Flanagan

Things You Never Knew Existed
Josh Olsen